First published as *Wondere wereld: Sterren en planeten* in Belgium and Holland by Clavis Uitgeverij, Hasselt—Amsterdam, 2017
English translation from the Dutch by Clavis Publishing Inc., New York

Visit us on the Web at www.clavisbooks.com.

Mack's World of Wonder: Stars and Planets written and illustrated by Mack van Gageldonk

ISBN 978-1-60537-381-2

This book was printed in April 2018 at Publikum d.o.o., Slavka Rodica 6, Belgrade, Serbia.

First Edition
10 9 8 7 6 5 4 3 2 1

Mack's **world of WONDER**

STARS AND PLANETS

Mack

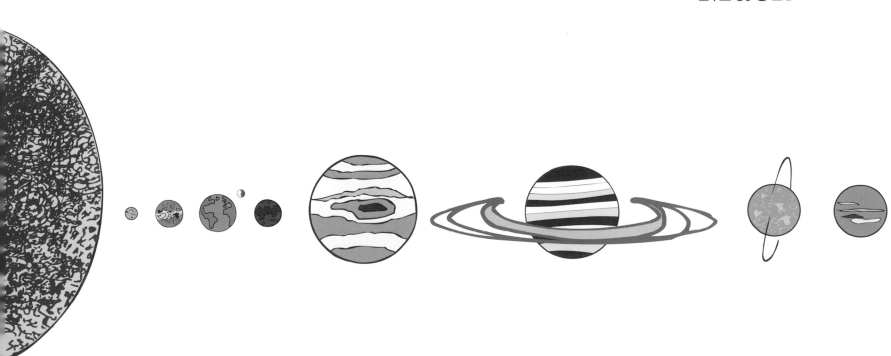

Clavis
NEW YORK

CONTENTS

THE EARTH

The earth is our home. From where we stand, the earth looks flat and enormous. But from space, the earth looks very different. The earth is not flat but a round ball, and it looks much smaller from a distance. There are several balls floating in space. We call them planets.

The earth is sometimes called "the blue planet." From outer space you can see white and brown-greenish spots on and around the earth, but the biggest part of our planet is blue, the color of the seas and oceans.

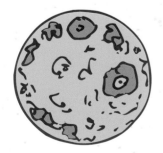  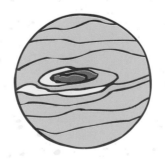  

Which planet is the earth?

The sun is not a planet but a star. A star is round like a planet, but much bigger. Stars give off a lot of light and are burning hot. The sun provides warmth and light to the earth.

The sun doesn't shine directly on the earth. Its beams are filtered by a thick layer of air called the atmosphere. This way, it gets warm on Earth but never too hot.

Thanks to the sun, lots of things can live on Earth.
Which animal do you think is getting a little hot here?

THE EARTH AND THE SUN

Since the earth spins around, it appears that the sun is in a different place every moment of the day. At night when it is dark, the sun is nowhere to be seen. The sun helps us know what time it is. If the sun is high up in the sky, it's about noon. When the sun is low and the sky turns red, day is turning into evening.

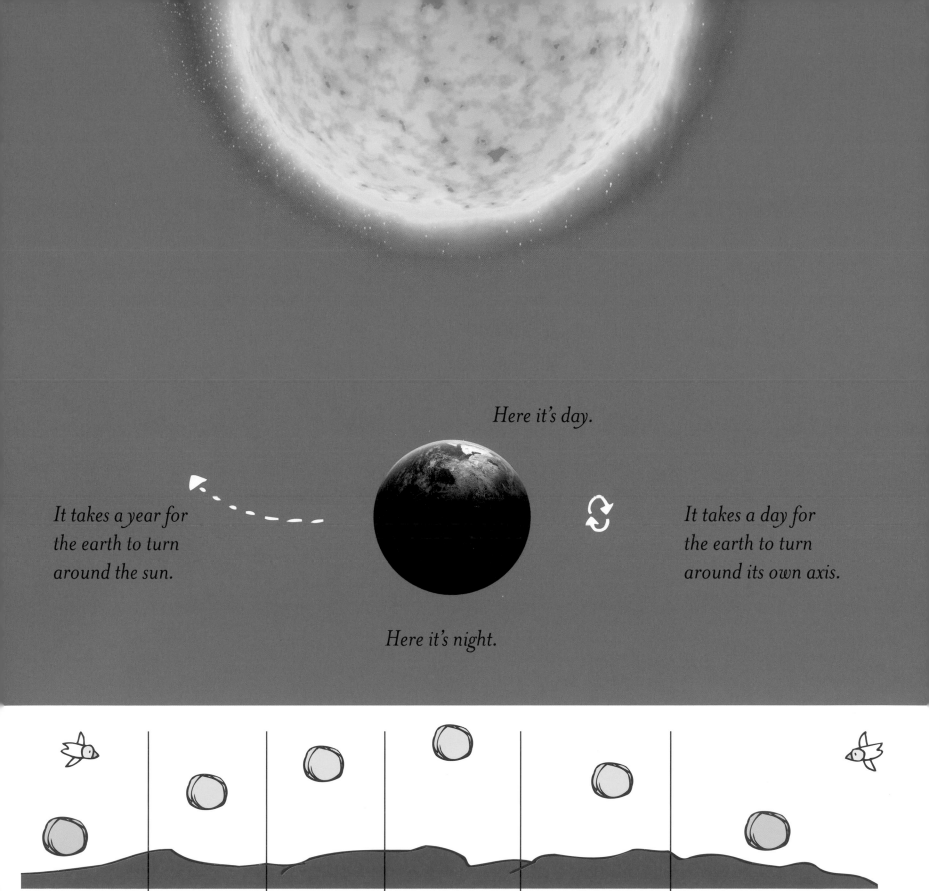

Here it's day.

It takes a year for the earth to turn around the sun.

It takes a day for the earth to turn around its own axis.

Here it's night.

Which picture shows the sun at noon?

THE EARTH AND THE MOON

When the sun sets, we see something else in the sky from Earth: the moon. The moon is much smaller than the sun and even smaller than the earth. It looks big from the earth because it's closer to us. Even though the moon is smaller than Earth, it has great power. It pulls at the earth like a strong magnet. Look at the seas and oceans. With the moon above the ocean, the water is higher than usual: it's high tide. And when the moon is not above the ocean, the water is low: it's low tide!

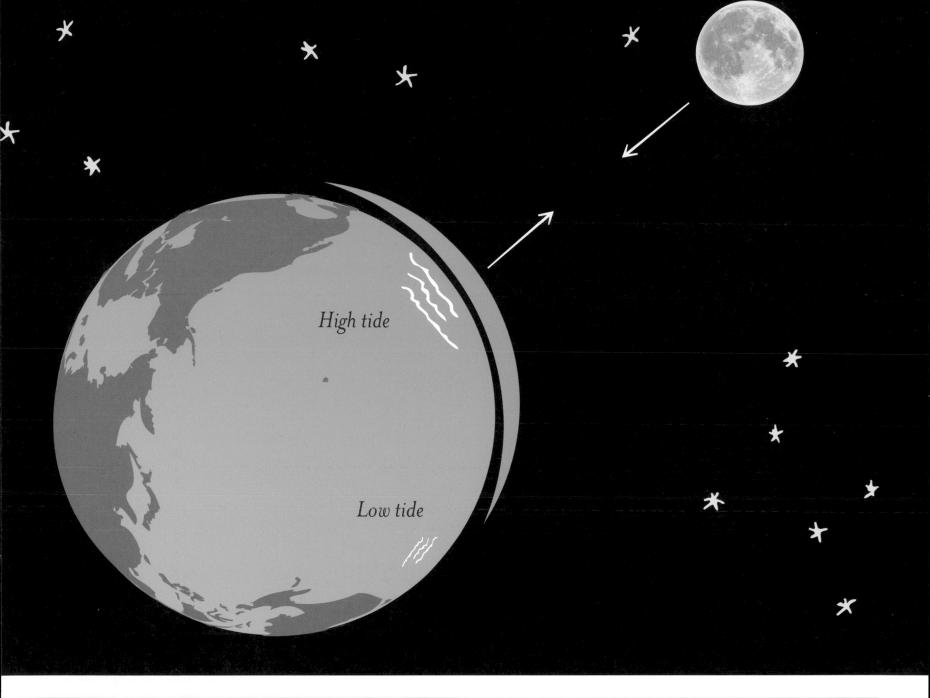

High tide

Low tide

Where is it low tide? And where is it high tide?

THE EARTH AND THE MOON

The moon looks different every day. Sometimes you can see all of it, like a round pie in the sky. Sometimes it looks like a half-circle. Sometimes it looks like a little banana in the sky. Sometimes you don't see it at all! This is because of the sun. When the sun lights the moon fully, you can see all of it. When the earth is in between the sun and the moon, sunlight shines on only a part of the moon.

When you can see the entire moon and it's at its largest, we call that a full moon. A week later it's a half-moon. Another week later the moon is fully dark. Then it's a new moon. After that it's half full and finally full again. The progression of full moon to the next full moon takes about thirty days. That's where month got its name!

Where is the moon full and where is the moon half full?

THE STARRY SKY

You can see them only when it gets dark, but they're always there: the stars. When the sky is clear at night, you can see thousands. The sky looks lit up by all those tiny glowing lights. In reality, those tiny dots of light are not small at all. They are often much bigger than our sun and they give just as much or more light. Stars just look that small because they are incredibly far away.

Long ago, ships would use the starry sky to find their way. Captains knew when and where they could see a star in the sky. Planets can help with directions as well. Venus is the biggest dot in the sky, and Mars looks red.

Do you recognize Mars?

STAR SIGNS

Have you ever looked at the starry sky at night? By connecting the stars, you might recognize a triangle, a heart, or maybe even an animal or a part of a face. Humans have been seeing pictures in stars for ages. They have discovered a bull, a fish, a big bear, a small bear, and even twins in the stars. Do you know what these pictures are called? Constellations!

Constellations are made by connecting the stars.
Here are Capricorn, Scorpio, and Gemini.

Do you recognize Pisces, Gemini, and Taurus?

COMETS

Once in a while, what looks like a white ball with a tail behind it travels through the sky. That's a comet. Comets are chunks of ice, snow, and rock that float through space. When they come too close to the sun, they melt. The tail is actually a kind of trail that a comet leaves behind. Few comets fly by the earth. A while ago the comet Hale-Bopp passed by Earth, and it will return in about two thousand years!

Hale–Bopp was clearly visible in the sky for one year and a half.

Which of these flying balls do you think is a comet?

METEORS

Meteors are also sometimes called falling stars. Yet falling stars actually have nothing to do with stars. They are typically rocks that head toward the earth at high speed. Usually, they burn up in the sky because the earth is protected by the atmosphere. The rocks light up and that's why it looks like a star is falling!

Sometimes meteors are so large they don't burn completely in the atmosphere. Their remains crash into the earth. Then they are called meteorites. Meteorites can create big craters, like this Wolfe Creek Crater in Australia.

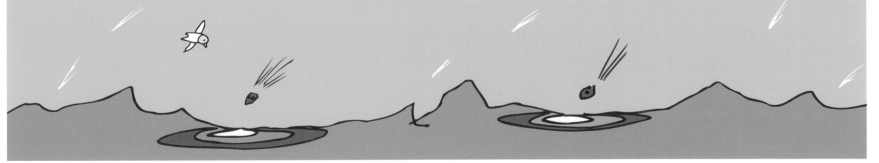

Which meteors didn't burn up in the sky?

POLAR LIGHTS

If you were on the North or the South Pole and looked up at night, you might be amazed by the polar lights. The polar lights are charged particles of the sun that bounce into the atmosphere, releasing energy, which results into a beautiful light show.

The polar lights come in all kinds of shapes and colors. It may be the biggest light show on Earth.

Are the polar lights visible when it's dark or when it's light?

SOLAR ECLIPSE

On rare occasions, the moon comes right between the earth and the sun. When that happens, in some locations it gets dark in the middle of the day, just like nightfall. But moments later the moon moves and the sun quickly appears again. This phenomenon is called a solar eclipse. To watch a solar eclipse, you have to put on special glasses. People travel from all over of the world to the place where the solar eclipse is best visible.

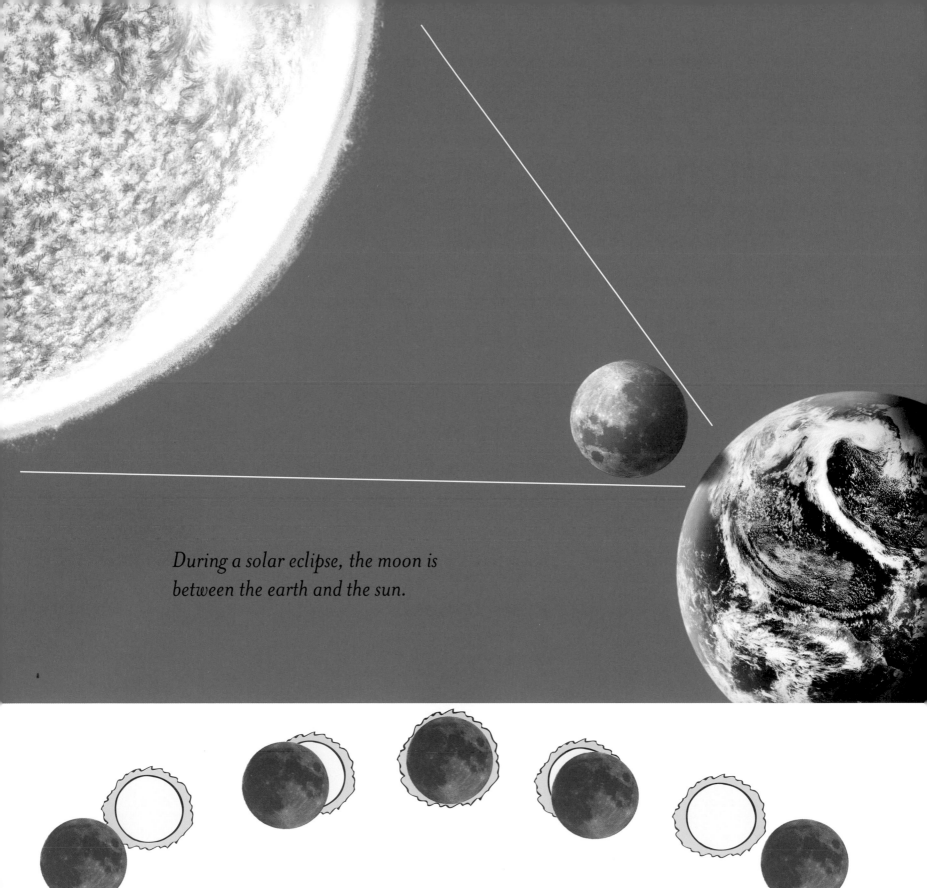

During a solar eclipse, the moon is between the earth and the sun.

Which picture shows the sun almost completely hidden by the moon?

OUR SOLAR SYSTEM

The earth is not the only planet. Eight planets orbit around the sun, just like the earth. Along with the sun, the eight planets form the solar system. The names of the planets, in order from the sun, are Mercury, Venus, Earth, Mars, Jupiter, Saturn, Uranus, and Neptune.

Mercury, Venus, Earth, Mars, Jupiter, Saturn, Uranus, and Neptune orbit around the sun.

Can you figure out which two planets are in the wrong order?

THE SUN

The sun, the star in the middle of our solar system, is much, much bigger than the planets. It's almost a hundred times bigger than all the planets put together. Because the sun is so close, a lot of planets in the solar system get its heat and light. Without the sun, it would be dark and ice cold.

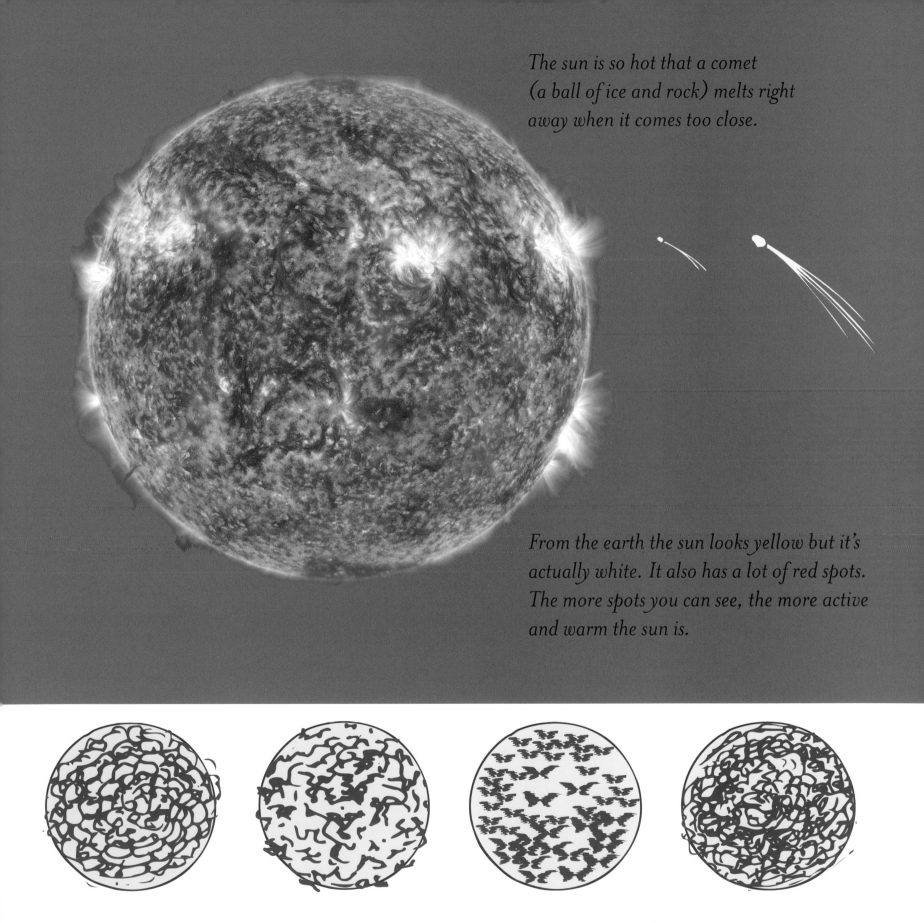

The sun is so hot that a comet (a ball of ice and rock) melts right away when it comes too close.

From the earth the sun looks yellow but it's actually white. It also has a lot of red spots. The more spots you can see, the more active and warm the sun is.

Which picture shows sun spots that are shaped like a butterfly?

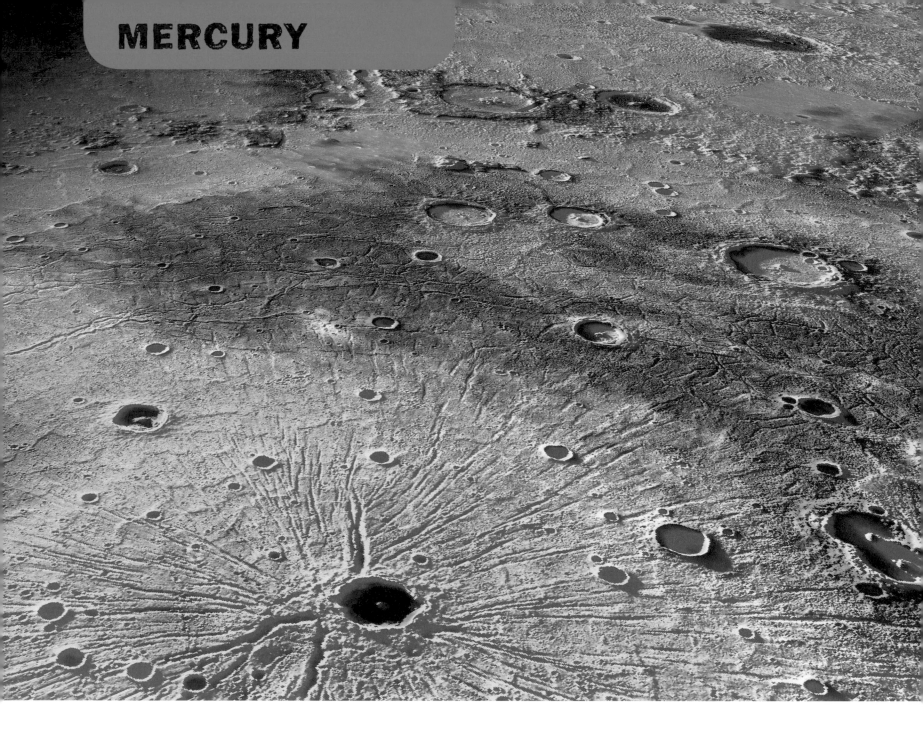

MERCURY

Mercury is the closest planet to the sun. From Mercury, the sun seems much bigger than the earth. By day it can be very hot. Very, very hot. With temperatures higher than 750 degrees Fahrenheit a rocket ship would melt! The surface of Mercury has a lot of craters and holes. They were created by volcanic eruptions and the impact of big chunks of rock (meteorites).

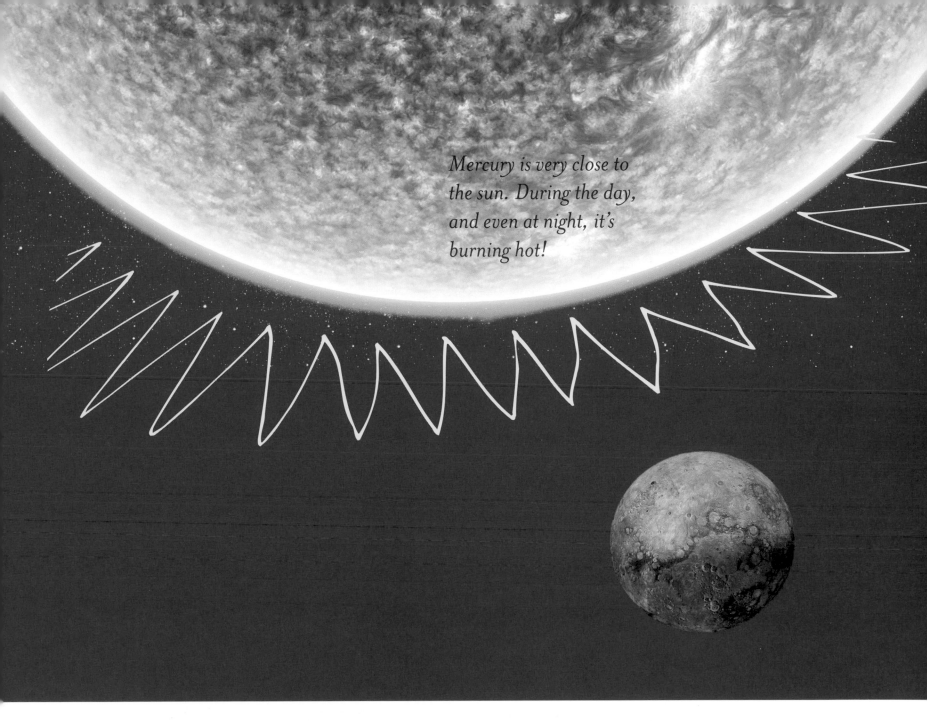

Mercury is very close to the sun. During the day, and even at night, it's burning hot!

Which planet is Mercury?

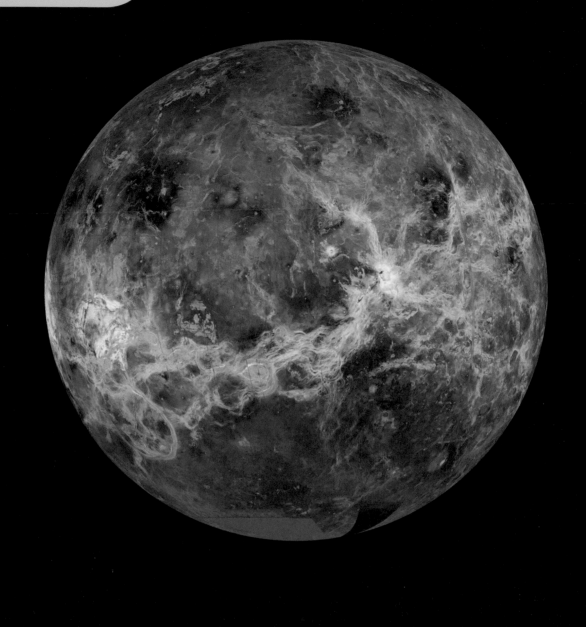

Venus is the second planet from the sun. A lot of clouds float around the planet. The clouds are made of droplets of toxic gases, not water, like on Earth. Venus may be the earth's neighbor, but we definitely cannot live there. When it rains on Venus, the droplets from the gases would burn your skin! You would also choke on the toxic fumes. And it's even hotter than on Mercury.

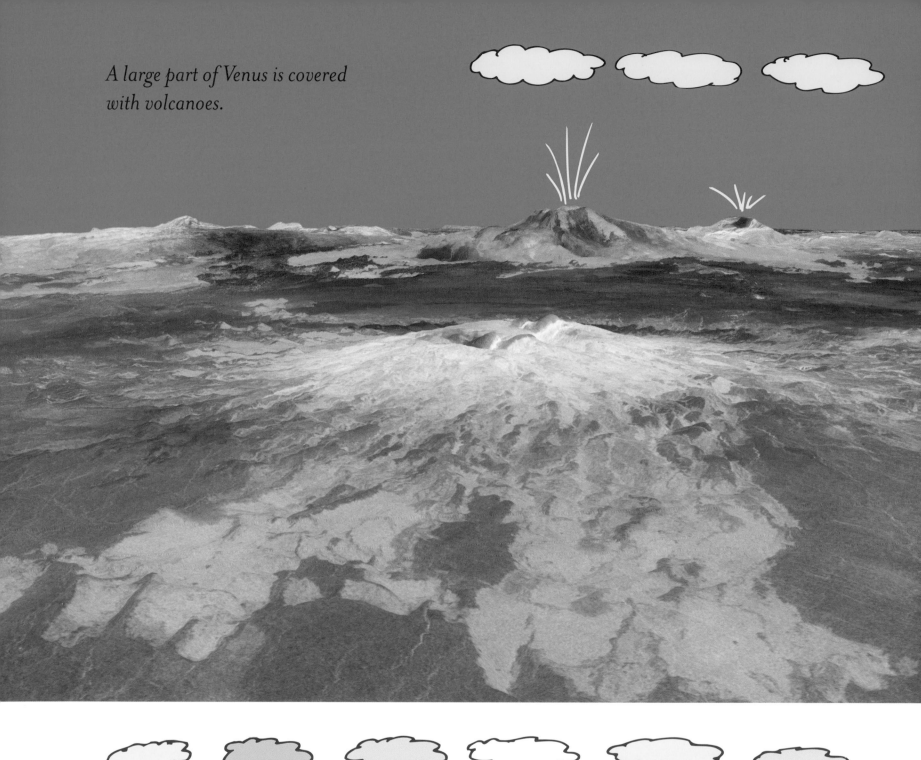

A large part of Venus is covered with volcanoes.

Which color of clouds won't you find on Earth?

Earth is the third planet from the sun. On Earth, it's not as hot as on Mercury and Venus, nor as cold as the planets that are farther away from the sun. That's why we can live here quite nicely. Seen from space, the earth looks beautiful, with its blue oceans, white clouds, and green landmasses.

Earth is the only planet in the solar system where life exists. It's warm and there's oxygen to breathe and water to drink. It's perfect!

Which planet is Earth?

The moon doesn't revolve around the sun, but around the earth. The surface of the moon is very rough. There are volcanoes and mountain chains. Meteorites have created a lot of holes in the moon. The moon is much smaller and lighter than the earth, so gravity works differently there. Astronauts have noticed that when they walk on the moon, every step feels like a kangaroo jump.

Everything is much lighter on the moon than on Earth. Astronauts can easily pick up heavy rocks.

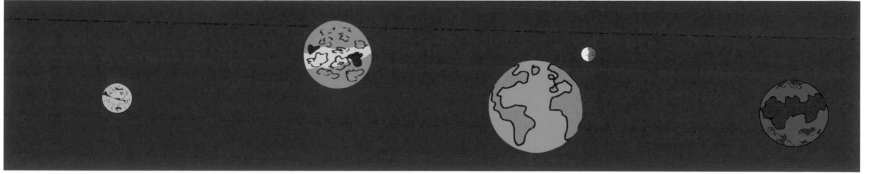

Can you spot the moon?

MARS

Mars is also called the red planet. There is a lot of iron on Mars and there used to be a lot of water. Iron and water create rust, and that gives the planet its unique rusty color. Mars is just a little farther from the sun than the earth. It's also colder there. On the warmest days it's sometimes seventy degrees Fahrenheit, but on cold days it can be a hundred degrees below zero. Brrr!

The sky from Mars doesn't look blue, like on Earth, but orange or pink. Two moons float in the sky, Phobos and Deimos. These aren't big and round, but very small and bumpy. They look like potatoes.

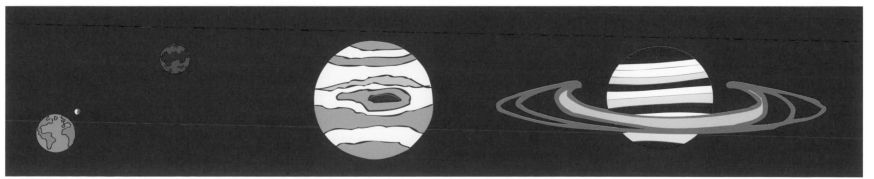

Which planet is Mars?

JUPITER

Jupiter is the biggest planet in the solar system. It's more than a thousand times the size of the earth. Jupiter is recognizable by its orange spot. Scientists have learned that the orange spot is a storm: a giant hurricane! The hurricane is much larger than the earth. Will the storm soon pass? Probably not, because it's been raging on Jupiter for more than three hundred years!

The biggest planet in our solar system also has the biggest moon. The moon Ganymede is very large: even bigger than the planet Mercury.

The moon Io is yellow, orange, and red and looks like a pizza.

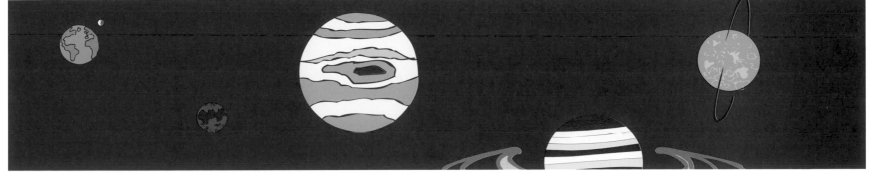

Which planet is Jupiter?

After Jupiter, **Saturn** is the second-largest planet in our solar system. The rings around the planet are remarkable. That's why Saturn is also called the Ring Planet. The rings consist of millions of pieces of ice and rocks. They float around Saturn, along with sixty-five moons. One of those moons is called Titan. Titan is as big as a planet and has an air layer around it, just like Earth. Though it's very cold there, some scientists believe that life could be possible on Titan.

Saturn has sixty-five moons!

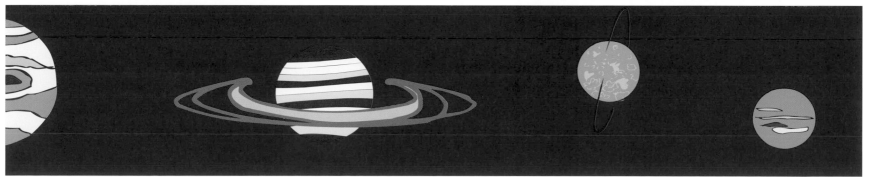

Which planet is Saturn?

URANUS

Uranus is the seventh planet from the sun. Only Neptune is farther away. You can't see Uranus without a telescope or a space probe. A space probe is a specialized spacecraft that takes measurements and makes photos. It takes nine years for a probe to reach Uranus. Uranus is extremely cold. The whole surface is one layer of ice.

Uranus has rings like Saturn. The rings of Uranus are thin and go from top to bottom.

Uranus has many moons, and almost all are named after characters from famous stories. One moon is called Juliet, after the character from the play Romeo and Juliet.

Which planet is Uranus?

Neptune is the planet farthest away from the sun. It's extremely cold there and very windy. Wind speeds of five times the most powerful tornado on Earth have been recorded.

Neptune is the last planet in our solar system. Pluto floats even farther away from the sun in space, but that heavenly body is so small that scientists don't consider it a real planet. They call Pluto a dwarf planet. There are more dwarf planets in our solar system, but Pluto is the best known.

Which planet is Neptune?

THE UNIVERSE

THE UNIVERSE

The universe consists of everything there is. If you add up all the stars, the planets, and all the space in between, you get the universe. No one has ever seen the end of the universe, or the beginning. It's that big. Pictures have been made with space telescopes of stars that are a billion times farther away than our sun. And even that's just a little piece of the universe. Incredible, right?

No one knows exactly how the universe came into being. Lots of scientists think that the universe started as something very small, but also something very heavy, like a kind of heavy dot. This exploded and, over a million years, all the stars and planets were shaped by the particles of dust that were released. They call that the Big Bang.

All of these things are part of our universe.

THE MILKY WAY

The group of stars that's closest to the earth is called the Milky Way. Our solar system is just a tiny part of the Milky Way. On a clear, dark night you might see a glimpse of the Milky Way as a strip of thousands and thousands of stars and clouds of gas. It looks endless! And to think that the universe contains not one or two star systems like the Milky Way, but millions or billions.

The universe consists of billions of star systems, in beautiful shapes and colors. One of them is the Milky Way.

Have you ever seen the Milky Way?

OTHER STARS AND PLANETS

Stars come in all sorts and sizes. There are yellow stars, white stars, clear blue stars, and red stars. The star in the picture is a red giant: that's a star that's on the verge of exploding. The star swells and turns red and huge. Think of this: If the sun weren't so hot, a plane would be able to fly all the way around it in 220 days. But a plane would need a thousand years to travel around some red giants. That's how big they can be!

Many planets float in space, in the Milky Way, and in other star systems. They're hard to see from the earth, because planets don't light up, but only reflect the light from the stars.

Which color of star is the biggest?

Nebulas consist of stars and stardust. Stardust looks like colored clouds, but in fact it's particles that come together and form a star. This is the Eagle Nebula. Beautiful, isn't it? This nebula looks like it has a face and can fly like an animal.

Cosmic nebulas come in all imaginable shapes and colors. They are all beautiful.

How do you think the Horsehead Nebula got its name?

SPACE TRAVEL

You can fly through space with a rocket ship. A rocket has a super-strong engine, strong enough to leave the earth and fly into space. Two of the most famous astronauts are a Russian named Yuri Gagarin and an American named Neil Armstrong. Gagarin was the first man in space and Armstrong was the first man on the moon. But neither of them was the first astronaut to circle the earth. That was Laika, a street dog from Moscow.

Life is very different in space than on Earth. Astronauts train very hard to get used to it. One thing they practice is floating, because that's what you do in space.

Which animal made the first space flight?

On July 16, 1969, the first astronauts flew to the moon. The *Apollo 2* was launched from Kennedy Space Center in the United States with a moon lander. Everyone in the world eagerly watched their television screens. Would the rocket ship get to the moon? Some test flights had failed. The countdown began . . . Ten, nine, eight, seven, six, five, four, three, two, one, blast-off!

Apollo 2 *reached the moon after a four-day trip—the moon lander landed on the moon's surface.*

This rocket is on its way to the moon!

THE MOON LANDING

On July 20, 1969, *Apollo 2* reached the moon. The astronaut Neil Armstrong descended the stairs of the moon lander and was the first person ever to set foot on the surface of the moon. He planted the American flag and walked on the moon with big, slow jumps. He drove a special moon vehicle. Then he flew back to Earth with some rocks he collected.

Neil Armstrong was the first human to set foot on the moon.

APOLLO 11

Which shoeprints look like astronaut footprints?

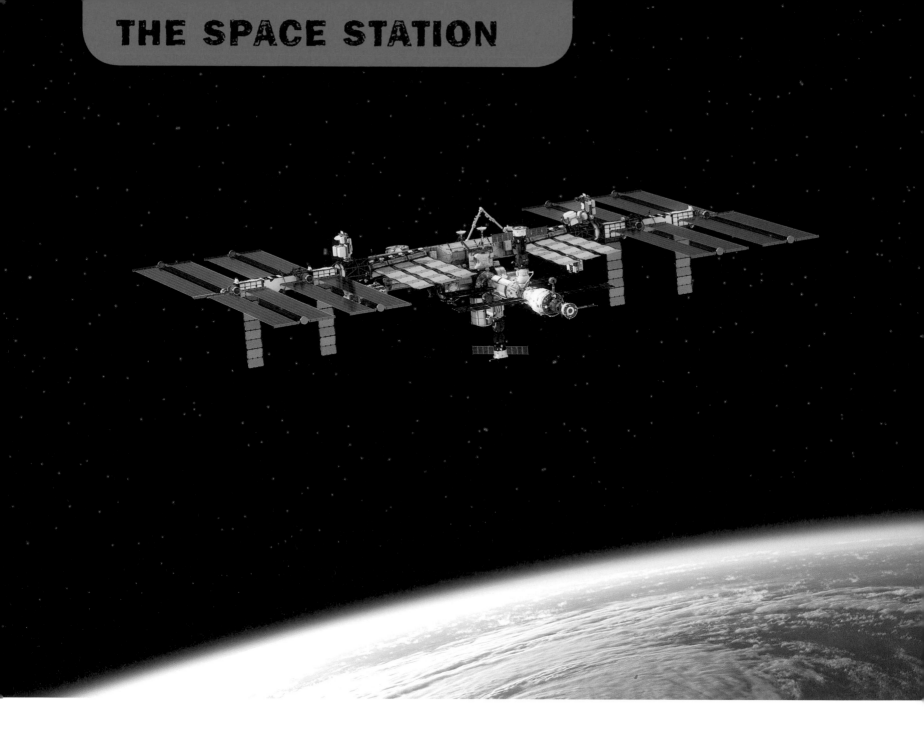

THE SPACE STATION

The International Space Station floats above the earth. In this space station, astronauts test what it's like to live in space for a long time. The crew members of the space station come from different countries. The astronauts mostly stay a few months, but some stay for more than a year.

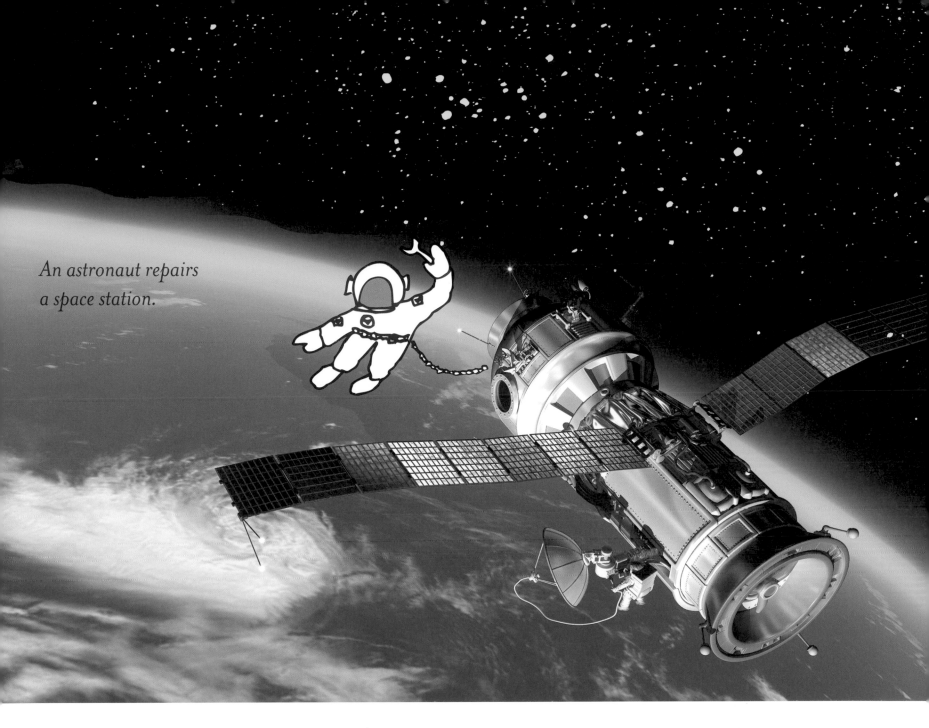

*An astronaut repairs
a space station.*

What do you see floating through the space station? 75

Space travel keeps improving. First rockets flew to the moon and now we're beginning to investigate the planet Mars. Hundreds of planets have been discovered with a telescope, most of them extremely far away.

Little is known about these far-off planets. What's the weather like? Can you breathe there? Are there plants, animals, and other creatures? And if there are, what do they look like? No one knows. But astronauts are curious. They want to discover everything, but there is so much more to learn!

Which planets are farthest away from Earth?